D1607212

ESCAPING
EAST GERMANY

BY BARBARA KRASNER

Published by The Child's World®
1980 Lookout Drive • Mankato, MN 56003-1705
800-599-READ • www.childsworld.com

Photographs ©: Chris Hoffmann/picture-alliance/dpa/AP Images, cover, 1; Shutterstock Images, 5, 10, 17; AP Images, 6, 9; akg-images/Binder/Newscom, 12; Kristof Lauwers/Shutterstock Images, 14; dpa/picture-alliance/dpa/AP Images, 18; Zentralbild/AP Images, 21; Manuel Fuentes Almanzar/Shutterstock Images, 22; Dieter Bauer/hl/str/AP Images, 24; Tobias Schwarz/Reuters/Newscom, 26; Karl Staedele/picture-alliance/dpa/Newscom, 28

ISBN 9781503825321
LCCN 2017959690

Printed in the United States of America
PA02377

TABLE OF CONTENTS

FAST FACTS 4

Chapter 1
URSULA HEINEMANN..............7

Chapter 2
WOLFGANG ENGELS.................13

Chapter 3
ESCAPE BY TUNNEL 19

Chapter 4
ESCAPE BY BALLOON.............25

Think About It 29
Glossary 30
To Learn More 31
Selected Bibliography 31
Index 32
About the Author 32

FAST FACTS

- After World War II (1939–1945), the winning **Allied powers** occupied Germany. Great Britain, France, and the United States controlled Germany's western section. The Soviet Union controlled its eastern section.

- In 1949, West Germany and East Germany formed. West Germany's capital city of Berlin lay in East Germany. Berlin was also divided into eastern and western sections.

- By 1957, East Germany put laws in place to punish people who tried to escape. The punishments included imprisonment and hard labor.

- The East German government built a wall between East and West Berlin in August 1961. The wall was meant to keep people from escaping. The first wall was built with barbed wire and cinder blocks. It was later rebuilt with concrete walls that were 15 feet (4.6 m) tall. It was protected by armed guards and mines.

- By the 1980s, the Berlin Wall extended 28 miles (45 km) through Berlin and 75 miles (121 km) around the western section of the city.

Parts of the Berlin Wall are preserved today at the Berlin ▶ Wall Memorial.

- Between 1961 and 1989, approximately 5,000 people managed to escape East Germany. At least 138 people died trying to escape.
- The Soviet Union collapsed in 1989, and the wall came down. Germany **reunified** in 1990.

Chapter 1

URSULA HEINEMANN

On the morning of August 13, 1961, 17-year-old Ursula Heinemann woke up at 4:45 a.m. She walked to a train station in East Berlin to catch the morning train. She had a waitressing job at the Plaza Hotel in West Berlin.

Each day, Ursula walked nearly 1 mile (1.6 km) to the train station from her family's apartment in East Berlin. But on that morning, the ticket collector announced that the border between East and West Berlin was closed. No trains were leaving for West Berlin. Ursula ran out of the station and down the street back to her family's apartment.

In the apartment, Ursula stayed glued to the radio and television for news. She learned that East German construction workers had begun to build a border wall between East and West Berlin the night before. The wall was made of barbed wire. Armed East German troops guarded the wall to keep people from escaping.

◀ **West Berliners look on as construction workers build the Berlin Wall in August 1961.**

Before the wall was built, many people had fled East Germany. Many sought better job opportunities in the West. This had threatened East Germany's **economy**. The wall was built to stop more workers from leaving East Germany.

In the days that followed, Ursula watched as the city became divided. Armed men guarded the bank of the Teltow Canal near her family's apartment. Guards in motorboats also patrolled the canal. They kept people from swimming across the canal to West Berlin. And along the border, workers began to make the wall more permanent. They replaced the barbed wire with concrete.

To make money, Ursula spent a day waitressing at a restaurant in East Berlin. There, she learned from border guards that they planned to shoot anyone who tried to cross the border. Ursula's heart sank. She wondered if she would ever be able to get back to West Berlin.

Ursula had regularly crossed the border into West Berlin before the wall went up. By working in West Berlin, she had been supporting West Germany's economy. Ursula's aunt and mother worried that the **Communist** East German government was suspicious of Ursula. They worried she was in danger. They urged her to escape to the West.

A police officer guards East Berlin workers as they increase ▶ the height of the Berlin Wall in 1961.

On the afternoon of August 19, Ursula took a walk with her mother. They crossed a bridge. A border **checkpoint** was located nearby. It was still open, but only one way. People could only cross from the West to the East.

EAST AND WEST BERLIN, 1961

BERLIN

FRENCH SECTOR

WEST

SOVIET SECTOR

EAST

BRITISH SECTOR

AMERICAN SECTOR

- - - - BERLIN WALL
———— SECTOR BORDER
O   CHECKPOINT

CHECKPOINT
CHARLIE

Ursula and her mother came to a deserted vegetable garden between East and West Berlin. Ursula walked on ahead of her mother until she spotted a gap in the wall. It was just wide enough for Ursula to squeeze through. This part of the wall was made up of barbed wire. The barbs tore at her sweater. But she slowly moved forward. She used one hand to lift the wire. The wire slashed her hand.

Ursula came across a second barbed wire fence. Although she was bleeding, she managed to lift the wire. She crawled underneath it.

Just ahead, Ursula could see the sign marking the border. She saw one guard but couldn't tell if there might be more. She crawled past the border sign. She didn't know whether the guard saw her or ignored her. Either way, he gave her no trouble.

Ursula arrived in West Berlin with only her identification card, a handkerchief, and the clothes on her back. She had to register with the West German authorities. Luckily, she already had a job in West Berlin. Her employer gave her a place to stay for free. Despite her good fortune, though, she had nightmares about her escape and separation from her mother.

Chapter 2

WOLFGANG ENGELS

On April 17, 1963, 19-year-old Wolfgang Engels sat in the driver's seat of an East German armored car. He announced to people nearby that he was going to escape East Berlin. Over the roar of the engine, he asked if anyone wanted to come along. But East Germans knew that people who attempted escape risked imprisonment or death from the armed border guards. Wolfgang was on his own. He revved the engine and aimed the vehicle toward the Berlin Wall.

Wolfgang had hatched his escape plan earlier in April 1963. One evening, Wolfgang and his friends had been walking near the Berlin Wall on the East German side. An East German soldier armed with a machine gun ordered them to stand against the wall and put their hands in the air. Wolfgang was outraged. He was in the East German army. He had helped to build the wall. He didn't think he or his friends should be treated that way. So he put his hands down. The soldier beat Wolfgang for disobeying him.

◄ **An East German border guard patrols along the Berlin Wall in an armored car.**

▲ **The Stasi held some people in prisons, where the prisoners were interrogated and tortured.**

Then the soldier forced Wolfgang and his friends into a truck. They were taken to an **interrogation** center to be questioned by the Stasi, the East German secret police. After a while, the Stasi let them go. But Wolfgang had decided by then that he was going to escape. He did not want to live in a place where he could be accused of a crime for no reason.

Wolfgang's mother didn't understand why he was angry. She was a Communist and a strong supporter of the Stasi.

She had brought Wolfgang to East Germany from West Germany when he was just ten years old. She believed that the Communist government was always right. Wolfgang knew she wouldn't support or help him. So he didn't tell her of his escape plan.

Wolfgang worked for the East German army as a driver. One day, he noticed that a fleet of armored cars had gathered for an upcoming military parade. These cars were common on the streets of East Berlin. No one would be suspicious of an armored car moving toward the Berlin Wall.

Wolfgang learned how to drive an armored car. He waited until the car drivers had left for dinner on the evening of April 17. Then he stole one of the armored cars. He did not think much about the risks he was taking. He just drove.

An officer ordered Wolfgang to stop. But Wolfgang ignored the order. He broke through a chained gate onto the streets of East Berlin. No one followed him.

When Wolfgang was near the Berlin Wall, he slammed his foot on the gas pedal. His target was the American sector of West Berlin at a point just south of Checkpoint Charlie.

The armored car could not fully break through the concrete wall. Wolfgang scrambled out. An East German border guard shot at him. One bullet hit Wolfgang's back and exited through his chest. He felt the blow of the bullet, but he was not stunned.

He was too focused to feel much pain. He took cover by the hood of the armored car. The bullets kept coming. One grazed his hand.

After a while, Wolfgang noticed that more bullets were passing by. But some of these bullets came from the West German side. They were helping him. Dodging the gunfire, he took off for the wall. He scrambled to the top of the wall with a bleeding hand and a hole in his chest. He reached the barbed wire that edged the top of the wall. A group of West Germans lifted him down to the other side. One man took off his belt to bind Wolfgang's wounded hand.

Wolfgang spent a few weeks in a hospital, healing from a collapsed lung. He wrote letters to his mother, but she never responded. Wolfgang did not know it at the time, but his mother was working for the Stasi. She was secretly turning all of his letters over to the Stasi.

CHECKPOINT CHARLIE

There were many crossing points along the Berlin Wall. One of these was called Checkpoint Charlie. This checkpoint was located on the eastern border of West Berlin, along the American sector. Only foreigners were allowed to cross through this checkpoint. But it was the site of many escape attempts.

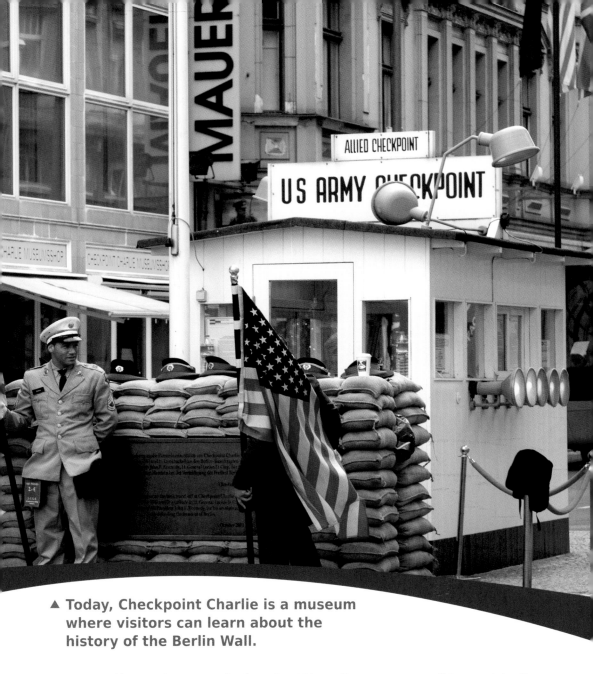

▲ Today, Checkpoint Charlie is a museum where visitors can learn about the history of the Berlin Wall.

Wolfgang later settled in the West German city of Dusseldorf, where he had been born. He rebuilt his life. He became a history and biology teacher.

Chapter 3

ESCAPE BY TUNNEL

On the night of October 4, 1964, East Germans arrived in groups of twos and threes at an apartment building in East Berlin. At the door of the apartment, each group whispered a code word: "Tokyo." The code word helped them get into the building. Behind the building and beneath an outhouse was a tunnel that would take them to West Berlin.

The tunnel had been the idea of 21-year-old engineering student Joachim Neumann. He and his friends met the escapees in the apartment and crossed their names off a list. Joachim held a gun in case they ran into any trouble. Their mass escape attempt was not without risks. Despite months of careful planning, Joachim knew they might be caught by the Stasi.

Earlier in 1964, Joachim had had one goal in mind: to get his girlfriend, Christa Gruhle, out of East Germany. Three years before, he had escaped himself using a borrowed Swiss passport. He had also brought his sister, hidden in a car, to West Germany.

◀ **Many people escaped from East to West Berlin through underground tunnels.**

THE STASI

The Stasi were the East German secret police. They were feared by many people in East Germany. Approximately 189,000 people were informants for the Stasi. Stasi informants spied on East Germans. It was not safe to voice opinions against the East German government in public or even at home. Punishments included imprisonment, torture, and death. The Stasi kept files on every person they thought to be suspicious.

Joachim and other university students then planned a way to help family and friends in East Germany escape.

Since Joachim's escape, the Berlin Wall had been built. Joachim and his friends decided to build a tunnel underneath the wall. This would allow people to escape undetected from East to West Berlin.

The first attempted tunnel escape failed. Someone informed the Stasi of their plan. The Stasi arrested them as they tried to escape through the tunnel. Christa was one of the people who was arrested. She received a 16-month prison sentence.

Joachim and his friends did not give up. They started digging another tunnel underneath an abandoned bakery in West Berlin. It took five months of digging to create a tunnel as long as a football field. On October 3, 1964, the tunnel was finally ready.

Joachim and the others sent word to family and friends in East Berlin. The escapees were told to come to the apartment.

▲ **An East German police officer investigates an underground escape tunnel in 1962.**

Fluchttunnel,
"Tunnel 57" 1964

Then they were supposed to come to the cellar door and give the password. They were told to take off their shoes and tiptoe to an inner courtyard that led to an outhouse. They had to be as quiet as possible. Border guards were stationed across the street. A helper was stationed in a tall building on the other side of the wall. The helper surveyed the streets around the apartment building. If there was trouble, the helper would shine a light to warn the escapees.

Once inside the outhouse, the escapees climbed down a ladder. This led through an opening in the floor to the tunnel. They moved through mud and water in the dark.

Christa was among the escapees. She had sent Joachim a note letting him know that the Stasi were letting her out of prison early. Joachim got a message to her. That night, Christa went to the apartment building.

The escapees crawled single file through the tunnel. When they reached the West Berlin bakery, helpers used ropes to pull them up to street level. Fifty-seven people escaped in this way over the course of two nights. The tunnel became known as Tunnel 57, named after the number of escapees. It was the largest single tunnel escape from East Germany.

◄ **The site of Joachim Neumann's escape tunnel is marked today by metal plaques at the Berlin Wall Memorial.**

Chapter 4

ESCAPE BY BALLOON

At around midnight on September 16, 1979, 37-year-old aircraft mechanic Hans Peter Strelczyk bumped along narrow roads in his small car. He was headed toward the spot he and 24-year-old bricklayer Günter Wetzel had scouted out. The forest clearing above the village of Possneck in East Germany would give them plenty of space for their escape. Hans Peter's wife and younger son, along with Günter's wife and two children, were crowded in the car.

This was the perfect night for their escape attempt. The winds were right. The car dragged along a small trailer, carrying their homemade hot-air balloon. Secured to the top of the car was a piece of canvas. It covered the balloon's basket and four tanks of gas. Günter and Hans Peter's 15-year-old son, Frank, followed along on a motorcycle.

Once they reached the clearing, Hans Peter, Günter, and Frank got to work. They unpacked all of the equipment from the trailer.

◄ **The Strelczyk and Wetzel families pose in September 1979 with the hot-air balloon they used to escape East Germany.**

▲ Hans Peter Strelczyk (far left) and his family visit an exhibit about their escape at the Berlin Wall Museum.

They anchored the balloon and the basket to the ground with ropes connected to an iron spike. Günter lit the **burner** while Hans Peter inflated the balloon. Then all eight of them scrambled into the balloon's basket. Günter and Frank cut the ropes.

The basket lifted off the ground. They then started to drift westward. Within ten minutes, they had soared to approximately 6,000 feet (1,830 m). Everything was going according to plan.

Hans Peter and Günter had been planning their escape for more than a year. The two men met and became friends in early 1978. They were both tired of living under a government that strictly controlled their opinions and actions. They decided in March 1978 that they and their families would escape.

Inspired by a television program about the history of ballooning, Hans Peter and Günter hatched the idea to flee East Germany by using a hot-air balloon. But neither knew how to build one. They studied pictures and experimented. Their first try was a flop. The fabric they stitched together would not accept enough air. They tested different kinds of fabric using a vacuum cleaner to see which ones could hold air properly. They calculated the size of the balloon.

Hans Peter and Günter's wives stitched together more than 60 pieces of fabric to create the balloon. A motorcycle engine and a car **exhaust** system were used to create a fan to inflate the balloon. Günter built the burner with stovepipe, hoses, and four gas containers. But their second try at a balloon also failed.

Günter began to have second thoughts. His wife worried about what might happen if they crashed or if they were caught.

▲ **Hans Peter and Günter's hot-air balloon was made from curtains, bedsheets, and many other kinds of fabric.**

The friendship between Günter and Hans Peter became strained. They did not agree about safety measures. They parted ways.

But Günter soon changed his mind. When Hans Peter asked him to help with a third attempt in January 1979, he agreed.

By September, their plan was finally in progress. But they knew their fuel supply would not last forever. As the balloon crossed the border, a searchlight filled the sky. But the light did not reach the escapees. The balloon crash-landed in a bush in a West German village at 2:40 a.m.

Hans Peter and Günter led their families to a nearby barn. The men wanted to scout the area. They were not sure whether they had managed to make it to West Germany. But Günter had injured his leg upon landing.

They spotted headlights. They feared the headlights belonged to an East German car. But they soon identified it as a West German police car. They had reached their destination. They were finally safe.

THINK ABOUT IT

- How do you think you would react if you woke up to find a wall dividing the city or town in which you live?
- What risks did East Germans face in trying to escape?
- Would you have attempted to escape East Germany if it meant leaving family behind?

GLOSSARY

Allied powers (AL-ide POW-urz): During World War II, the Allied powers were the countries that fought against Germany, Italy, and Japan. The United States, Great Britain, and France were among the Allied powers.

burner (BER-nuhr): A burner is the part of a hot-air balloon in which the fuel is placed. Günter Wetzel made a burner from stovepipe and other materials.

checkpoint (CHEK-poynt): A checkpoint is a point along a border where travelers are stopped for inspection. Checkpoint Charlie was one of eight crossing points along the Berlin Wall.

Communist (KAHM-yoo-nihst): A Communist is a member of a political system in which all economic and social activities are controlled by the state. Wolfgang Engels's mother was a Communist.

economy (ih-KAH-nah-mee): An economy is a system of money, goods, and services used by a country or nation. The flight of people from East to West Germany hurt East Germany's economy.

exhaust (ig-ZAHST): Exhaust is the gas that escapes from an engine. Hans Peter Strelczyk and Günter Wetzel used a car exhaust system to inflate their hot-air balloon.

interrogation (in-tayr-uh-GAY-shun): Interrogation is the act of asking a series of questions, usually to get someone to reveal key information. Wolfgang Engels and his friends were questioned by the Stasi at an interrogation center.

reunified (re-YOO-nih-fyd): When something is reunified, it is joined back into a single thing. Germany reunified, or became a single country again, in 1990.

TO LEARN MORE

Books

Coddington, Andrew. *Germany*. New York, NY: Cavendish Square, 2017.

Cummings, Judy Dodge. *Great Escapes: Real Tales of Harrowing Getaways*. White River Junction, VT: Nomad Press, 2017.

Simmons, Walter. *Germany*. Minneapolis, MN: Bellwether Media, 2011.

Web Sites

Visit our Web site for links about escaping East Germany: childsworld.com/links

Note to Parents, Teachers, and Librarians: We routinely verify our Web links to make sure they are safe and active sites. So encourage your readers to check them out!

SELECTED BIBLIOGRAPHY

Cate, Curtis. *The Ides of August: The Berlin Wall Crisis—1961*. New York, NY: M. Evans & Company, 1978.

Mitchell, Greg. *The Tunnels: Escapes under the Berlin Wall and the Historic Films the JFK White House Tried to Kill*. New York, NY: Crown Publishing Group, 2016.

Sheffer, Edith. *Burned Bridge: How East and West Germans Made the Iron Curtain*. New York, NY: Oxford University Press, 2011.

Taylor, Frederick. *The Berlin Wall: A World Divided, 1961–1989*. New York, NY: HarperCollins, 2006.

INDEX

Berlin Wall, 4, 5, 7–8, 11, 13, 15, 16, 20

Checkpoint Charlie, 10, 15, 16
checkpoints, 10, 16

East Berlin, 4, 7, 8, 10
East Germany, 4, 5, 8, 20
Engels, Wolfgang, 13–17

Gruhle, Christa, 19, 20, 23

Heinemann, Ursula, 7–8, 10–11

Neumann, Joachim, 19–21, 23

Soviet Union, 4, 5
Stasi, 14, 16, 19, 20, 23
Strelczyk, Hans Peter, 25–29

Tunnel 57, 23

West Berlin, 4, 7, 8, 10
West Germany, 4, 8
Wetzel, Günter, 25–29
World War II, 4

ABOUT THE AUTHOR

Barbara Krasner is the author of more than 20 history books for young readers. As a German major in college, she spent a year studying in West Germany and visited both West and East Berlin, going through Checkpoint Charlie.